Neckties, Bo Squares

A Practical Guide To Upgrading Your Look!

2015 Edition

By Mark Davids

Table of Contents

Bow Ties

Pocket Squares

From the Author

Dear reader,

thank you for buying this book!

With this book you actually get 3 books in 1. It is a compilation of all 3 of my books, each covering a different piece of men's accessories:

- *Neckties - A Practical Guide to Buying, Tying, Wearing and Caring for Neckties*
- *Bow Ties – A Practical Guide*
- *Pocket Squares for Men – The Complete Guide.*

Ties have been in our culture for generations. Our grandfathers wore them, our fathers wore them. Every day you see businessmen, politicians, TV hosts and other influential men wearing them.

Why is this piece of cloth around men's necks so important? How did it come into our culture and why has it stayed here for so long when it seemingly has no practical value?

For years now, many have proclaimed that neckties are going extinct and that their days are long gone. But it doesn't seem to be going that way at all - quite the opposite is true: both neckties and bow ties are becoming more and more popular, especially in the casual sphere of men's clothing.

Apart from bringing a dash of formality and class into the casual menswear, ties are one of the few pieces with which men can accessorize their appearance. We men can put on a nice watch, glasses (if you wear them) and a tie – and that's about it. If these are the only options a man has to add a little flair to his attire, why should he not make the best use of the tie?

Everyone is talking about bow ties lately – fashion blogs around the world are promoting them, they are being featured on the most popular TV shows and they are often trending on Twitter. It didn't take long before they started appearing on your favorite actors and singers, and possibly even on the necks of some of your more daring and fashion forward friends! Is it time for you to jump aboard this train?

I believe that after you have integrated bow ties into your wardrobe, there's no reason why they cannot become the perfect day-to-day accessory, giving you an extremely individualized, adaptable and chic look.

The third piece of men's accessories we cover in this book are pocket squares. By wearing a pocket square in your suit or blazer breast pocket, you can elevate your style quickly. With an investment of some $20, you can separate yourself from the crowd!

Why not try it yourself?

The tips in this book are very practical; there is some theory explained, but it will be kept to the bare minimum. The purpose of the advice presented here is for you to absorb it quickly and take action.

Enjoy the reading as well as the results after the implementation of learnings from this book!

Mark Davids

Mark Davids

Neckties

A Practical Guide to Buying, Tying, Wearing and Caring for Neckties

2015 edition

About Neckties

1. Where Do Neckties Come From?

Neckties as we know them today, have been around since the 1650s, in different shapes and sizes. The history of neckties goes back much further though, back to the 3rd century BC where they were worn by Chinese warriors, as a way to protect their necks from cold weather. As with so many other things in life, neckties existed for centuries only in military use before being adopted by the masses.

The story of neckties gets interesting with the Croatians

Croatian soldiers with neckties as worn in 17th century

The story begins in the 1650s when Croatian troops, who were fighting for King Louis XIII, started wearing knotted scarf-like neckties that would eventually be called 'cravats.' The troops wore neckties for the same reason as their Chinese predecessors centuries before: to protect them from cold. Because of the Croats' success in the field, they caught the attention of the King and his military cohorts, and the 'cravat' was soon associated with the victories of the Croatian troops. At that time, no one but the Croatians wore anything similar. Very soon, the new trend caught on when French *fashionistas* took this detail and incorporated it into their style - and the bright future of neckties began!

From the 17th to the 20th century, many different styles of neckties took a central place in the wardrobe of the contemporary, fashionable man. From Macaronis to Incroyables, from bow ties to ascots, the necktie was evolving and taking on many shapes and sizes. It became what we know today in the early 20th century.

In 1924, a New Yorker named Jesse Langsdorf patented the design the modern necktie. We still use the same system and design to this day.

Along with neckties, the bow tie has also seen a recent surge in popularity. Bow ties also descended from the cravat and came onto the scene somewhere around the end of the 19th century when, for practical reasons, much smaller ties were required. Since its birth, the bow tie existed in many forms and sizes as well: floppy, stiff, geometric, bigger, smaller, until the beginning of the 20th century when the bow tie, as we know it today, came onto the scene and stayed.

2. Why Do Men Wear Neckties?

So, if we set aside all the cultural and symbolic reasons why men, after so many centuries still wear neckties, the question often asked is what is the purpose of that piece of fine cloth around our necks?

Why do men put up with all the knotting and unknotting, matching of colors and spending of money on them when there is no obvious functional reason to wear them?

A necktie does not keep you warm, nor does it cover any body part. The main reason why most men wear neckties today is professional - for many men the necktie is a required part of their professional wardrobe.

Are there any functional and practical reasons why men still wear neckties? Frankly, there are not many, but here are a few:

- Both neckties and bow ties keep your shirt collars neatly in place, preventing them from sagging or becoming misshapen.

- With the shirt collar lifted, buttoned up and secured with a necktie, your neck is covered, and thus protected from cold (at least a bit).
- A necktie hides the gaps between your shirt buttons so the professional look is protected (no exposed skin or body hair peeking out).
- In some cases, a necktie shows affiliation to a club or organization - either by a unique design (such as the repp neckties of many European universities) or a logo on the front of the necktie (as part of some companies' uniforms).

There you have it… not many practicalities, but enough that you can't say that neckties are just a useless accessory akin to jewelry. Could it be that men are, after all, fond of accessorizing, even if they don't admit it? **Together with a watch and glasses, a necktie is one of the rare pieces a man can use to accessorize his outfit.**

Buying Neckties

3. How to Buy a Necktie You Will Love for Years to Come

If you are like a majority of men, you probably have plenty of neckties hidden somewhere in your closet, but wear only a couple of them on a regular basis.

Why not take a different approach next time you go shopping for neckties: buy fewer neckties, but ones that you'll wear often and for a long time!

First, what you need to look for in a necktie is its quality. <u>There are 5 simple tests by which you can assess the quality of a necktie:</u>

<u>First</u> of all, high quality neckties are made of material that is cut at a 45 degree angle. On neckties where the ribbing, or knit, can be seen by the naked eye, you only need to look at it and notice if the diagonal stripes run at 45 degrees. On neckties where this is not visible, hold the necktie by the narrow end, and let it dangle for a moment. It should dangle completely straight, without any twisting.

Good quality neckties should fall completely straight, without twisting.

Second, check the necktie's elasticity by holding it at both ends and pulling – any good necktie will immediately return to its original length.

Third, make sure that a necktie has a 'slip stitch' by looking under the back seam of the necktie's shell. The slip stitch is the long vertical stitch up the back of the necktie, and on a high-end necktie, this will be hand-stitched. The slip stitch guarantees that the necktie will have some room to play and 'breathe', so that the stitching and material are not damaged from repeated tying and untying.

The 'slip stitch' guarantees that the necktie will have some room to play and 'breathe.'

Fourth, verify that the two seams that secure the lining at each end of the necktie are securely sewn. These guarantee the lateral stability of the surface of a necktie.

Finally, lightly pull the necktie's shell (lining) to make sure it does not move or wobble.

All five tests can easily be done in the shop in seconds. When buying online, buy only at reputable online shops that do these tests for you.

After quality, the next consideration is versatility: can the necktie be worn with a large percentage of your shirts and suits? Darker colors with stripes or another pattern in contrasting colors are always a wise choice. If you choose classic patterns and colors, your necktie will be more versatile and you will wear it more often. Colors like gray, dark blue, and red are quite good for that purpose and will coordinate nicely with many outfits.

Last but not least, take notice of the necktie's size. Although most neckties come in standard sizes, people of shorter, taller, or larger build should spend time finding a size that fits them. If you are shorter, choose shorter neckties around 55 inches or 140 cm. If you are taller or larger, choose longer neckties - more than 59 inches or 150 cm. When tied, the necktie should reach the belt buckle, and not have too much excess length on the back blade.

The width of the necktie, though largely determined by contemporary fashion trend, should be matched with a suit jacket's lapels. Wider lapels call for a wider necktie, and narrower lapels or slim suits call for a narrower necktie. The gold standard of today is a width of approximately 3 inches or 8 cm.

By taking quality, versatility, and size into consideration when buying neckties, you will wear them often, and look stylish for years to come. Enjoy all the extra attention you will get!

4. Beware of Cheap Neckties!

Cheap neckties can be found in many shops, online or off, but the real challenge can be to find inexpensive, yet high-quality neckties.

As someone wise once said "I am not rich enough to buy cheap things." If you want to save money, cheap neckties might be attractive at first. But by buying on price point alone, you are considering only the initial investment. What about the maintenance costs, the product's lifetime value, its quality, the image it exudes, etc.?

Cheap neckties can negatively affect your reputation

Today people associate themselves with their favorite brands and are very sensitive to what kind of image their brand projects to the world around them. In the world of menswear, wearing cheap neckties can tarnish your whole look and even your reputation. Wearing a necktie is a cultural symbol, a sign of respect and respectability, and wearing a cheap necktie ruins that symbolism.

„Wearing no necktie at all is better than wearing an obviously cheap necktie!"

How do you recognize high quality neckties?

First, they should be made of natural material or a blend of natural materials: silk, wool or cotton. Beware of synthetic materials like polyester. Synthetic neckties are usually the cheapest; they will not make nice-looking knots and will crease more. People will notice this.

A good necktie will feel sturdy and thick. This is something that is difficult to describe in writing, but with time and experience you will recognize a good quality necktie simply by feeling it in your hand. You should check that all stitches are done well and hold the fabric securely together.

Finally, do the 5 simple tests explained in Chapter 3 to inspect the quality of the necktie.

With these few tests you can quickly determine if the necktie is just cheap or a good deal. Take a pass on cheap neckties that are cheap for a reason.

And what about cheap bow ties?

Similar criteria can be applied to bow ties. You should again look only for natural materials, and make sure that the bow tie is well-crafted and well-stitched. With bow ties, pay more attention to the size. Make sure it fits your collar, and make sure the bow itself is not too big (you don't want to look like a clown) nor too thin. Bow ties are still uncommon enough that wearing a standard size is advisable; opting for a more unusual size might be a bit too much for many occasions.

In sum, finding a good deal on a necktie is a matter of knowing what to look for. Don't fall into trap of buying something just because it is cheap. Cheap ties can cost you more than just the purchase price. Make your image and reputation a major consideration when looking at a necktie's price tag!

5. Why Choose Silk Over Other Materials?

Let's face it, silk neckties are more expensive than neckties made of other materials, except maybe poplin or cashmere. In the world of neckties, silk is the best way to go, and silk has always been an expensive material.

What is it about silk that makes it the best material for making great neckties?

Silk is THE fabric of choice for neckties

Since its discovery, silk has been considered the finest and most respected of all woven textiles. It was worn by the rich and powerful. The process of producing raw silk is complex and lengthy, this is the reason it commands the price it does. Silk-making was first mastered in China, before spreading to Korea and Japan and finally to Europe. Today, the finest silk comes from France, Italy, India and China.

One hundred percent silk is absolutely the best material for a necktie. Silk gives a necktie great texture and a soft and smooth feeling to the touch. Its thread is very strong and resistant to stretching. This elasticity allows the necktie to keep its shape after repeated tying and untying.

The most respected designers throughout history have used exclusively natural materials to make neckties. **Silk, cotton, wool** are all quality materials for necktie-making. A blend of these materials is also acceptable. You will not find any designer neckties today that are not made from these three basic fabrics.

Again, avoid neckties made of polyester or other synthetics. These are novelty materials that simply don't have the characteristics needed to make a quality necktie; they don't have the elasticity or strength of natural materials.

When you look for silk neckties, you will find the following three main types of silk:

- Woven silk - the pattern of the necktie is woven into the material of the necktie
- Printed silk - the pattern is printed onto the silk
- Knitted silk - usually a solid color with square end, its silk threads are machine knitted at a 90 degree angle.

Woven silk is the best fabric for silk neckties. The numerous ways of weaving the silk give woven neckties a vast array of different textures. Even the most detailed motif can be expressed with woven silk.

What to look for when buying silk neckties?

Quality is the most important aspect to consider when buying a necktie. Cheap neckties look cheap; in most cases you get what you pay for. With high-quality, designer silk neckties you can upgrade your look for much less than you would spend on a new suit. Synthetic neckties fall in the category of cheaper neckties, and as mentioned already, every good eye will immediately spot a polyester necktie on you. The money you save buying a polyester necktie will not offset the cheap image you risk exuding.

If you are in need of updating your necktie collection, look for high-quality neckties at a discount by shopping during the sales seasons. Necktie fashions do not change quickly; you don't need to fear buying a necktie only to have it be out of style next year. A quality necktie with a classic pattern will be a stylish and loyal companion for years to come.

If you spot a necktie that you like which would fit well into your collection, but is not yet discounted, don't wait. It will certainly cost less than a new suit or nice pair of shoes and has amazing potential for boosting your style.

6. Famous Designer Neckties You've Never Heard About!

When you think of designer neckties, you probably think of something like Armani or Hugo Boss - designers that do offer neckties, but just as a small part of their accessories selection. For these brands, neckties are just another product line. Typically they don't even handle designing or fabricating the neckties; this work usually goes to companies in Italy or China. The high prices these neckties command are dictated by the perceived value of the brand, not the tangible value or quality of the necktie itself.

But, there are many independent designers making extraordinary neckties.

Designer necktie makers that you will love

In France, the most famous neckties designer is Charvet. Charvet makes only handmade neckties and specializes in silk neckties. Their boutique in Paris offers the largest range of woven silk neckties in the world!

Another famous French designer of silk neckties is Hermes. It is difficult to pinpoint just one reason why a Hermes necktie is so special. Perhaps it is because of its inimitable style, or the power of the Hermes brand, or the beauty of the designs that come out twice per year under the Hermes brand name. Hermes neckties definitely attract attention to the wearer, and that might be worth their (high!) price.

Italy is famous for its designer neckties as well. One of the most respected makers of handmade neckties, with over 100 years of tradition, is Marinella. The highest standards of quality and service have made Marinella the epitome of good taste, in Italy and worldwide. A Marinella necktie is a lifetime investment!

While the Croatians were the first to wear the modern necktie's predecessor, they didn't develop a considerable necktie tradition or industry until recently. The French, Italian and English were more creative and entrepreneurial, but after Croatia gained independence in the early 1990s, a new brand – Croata – has emerged to revive Croatia's love for neckties.

All these brands also make designer bow ties. Wearing a bow tie will make you stand out from the crowd, but it is nice to see the bow tie slowly coming back into the mainstream. So, if you want to be ahead of the pack, pick up a quality bow tie and wear it proudly. Others will follow.

What makes designer neckties such a high quality garment?

The quality of designer neckties does not lie in the necktie's design itself, as anyone can design an interesting or eye-catching necktie. The designer's quality and reputation lies in many small details in the necktie production process. These small details have huge results; they ensure that the necktie will be durable, keep its shape and tie beautiful knots for many years to come! When you drop that extra money on a necktie from one of the designers listed above, this quality is what you are buying. All you have to do is choose a design you like.

7. Where to Shop for Neckties?

Neckties can be bought in many shops, offline or online. The benefits of buying neckties in brick-and-mortar stores are that you can try them on and get some advice from the sales personnel. Online however, you can easily shop around, compare prices and look at many different styles and designs in just a couple of minutes, all from your sofa or office. Since there are no sizes, buying your necktie online can be really simple and less expensive as well, as there are many good online shops competing for your attention and trust.

That said; if you want to visit some offline stores to see their offerings, don't miss Brooks Brothers, Macy's, Nordstrom, Barneys and other similar retailers selling men's clothing. You might check their websites as well.

There are many online retailers specializing in neckties that offer an excellent quality. Very often their neckties are made in limited quantities; therefore, you know you are buying exclusive products, often for very affordable prices.

Some online necktie retailers we shop at are:

http://www.dolbeau.ca/ - Canadian brand making exquisite neckties and bow ties with unique materials, all by hand. All their editions are very small and when sold out, they are gone.

http://www.generalknot.com/ - Neckties and bow ties, handmade in the USA with vintage fabrics. Every product comes with an exclusively numbered card, which means your tie will be a really unique piece!

http://www.bergbergstore.com/ - Norwegian brand making neckties (and other accessories for men) designed in Norway and hand made in Italy. Often they have very interesting designs.

http://www.etsy.com – a marketplace for many independent designers. Search their site for neckties and discover some great unique pieces made by designers from all over the world!

http://www.kentwang.com/ - small company from Austin, Texas that is dedicated to making high quality, classic menswear at reasonable prices. Check out their suits as well!

http://www.howardyount.com/ - founded in 2008, Howard Yount is dedicated to the uncompromising pursuit of style. Their goal is to provide high quality products with an attention to detail and high level of personal service.

http://www.drakes-london.com/ - founded in 1977, today Drakes is the largest independent producer of handmade neckties in England, offering also a wide range of shirts and pocket squares.

http://www.asuitablewardrobe.net/ - the clothing site for tailored men, combining award-winning editorial content with hand-made clothing and accessories from dozens of makers like Simonnot-Godard of France, Drake's London and Neapolitan makers. Like the great haberdashers of years past, it stocks products, such as braces, neckties and socks, in a wider range of sizes than is common elsewhere in the world, including made to measure versions of some items.

http://www.bensilver.com/ - offers classic, refined and tasteful clothing and accessories for gentlemen who enjoy the added dash of updated color. They present fresh collections of fine neckwear every season!

http://pierreponthicks.com/ - Mac and Katherine McMillan launched Pierrepont Hicks in 2009 out of a desire to make the perfect necktie. In the meantime they launched more products each season, including outerwear for both men and women, always remaining focused on accessories for life's travels, adventures and celebrations.

http://www.thetiebar.com/ - "Smart, stylish ties don't have to cost a fortune" – that's their motto. The Tie Bar offers vast selection of colorful and stylish pieces of men's accessories for extreme value prices (silk neckties for as low as $15!).

When shopping for high quality neckties, go for natural materials (silk, wool, cotton) and make sure that the necktie is well crafted and well-stitched together. People behind these websites are very knowledgeable about the origins of their products and would be happy to answer any of your questions. Look for a contact email and don't hesitate to email them with your inquiries.

Wearing Neckties

8. The Skinny on Skinny Neckties

Fashion styles come and go. Wide neckties will be popular for a time, then skinnier neckties will begin to take center-stage. After skinny neckties have enjoyed a period of popularity, then wide neckties again become chic... and so on.

The modern necktie, conceived by Jesse Langsdorf in 1920s, had basically the same measurements as today's necktie – around 3 inches (8 cm) wide across at the widest point and around 55 inches (140 cm) long - long enough to reach the belt of an average sized man after tying.

Over the years, designers have made several attempts to alter this standard. This is why we had wide neckties in the 1950s, narrow, square-ended neckties called 'ribbon neckties' in the 1960s, followed quickly by the other extreme - very wide neckties up to 6 inches (15 cm) wide.

These trends, thankfully, do not change too quickly, but on average each lasts around 10 years.

What's 'in' right now?

Today, the standard width of the necktie is considered to be 3 inches (8 cm), plus or minus half an inch. Anything narrower is considered a skinny necktie, any wider and it is a wide necktie.

So how should you decide whether to buy a skinny necktie or a wide one? Your best bet is to match the necktie to the lapels of your suit. A wider necktie is acceptable with broad suit lapels, and vice versa; a narrow necktie calls for narrower lapels and a skinnier, more tailored overall look. You should avoid wearing a necktie wider than the lapels of the suit jacket it is accompanying.

Your shirt collar should frame the necktie knot. Wider neckties generally make bigger knots and should be worn with shirts that have wider collars, such as 'spread collar' shirts. Skinny neckties make smaller knots and therefore are more suitable for smaller, narrower collars.

In any case, remember that the necktie knot should not lift the tips of the collar, and the knot should fit neatly into the triangle created by your buttoned shirt collar.

„In sum, when choosing your necktie, you should take into consideration the type of suit and shirt you will be wearing it with."

Author Mark Davids wearing Croata necktie

The optimum necktie size for you also depends on your build

If you are tall and skinny, a narrower necktie will look good on you. If you are of a bulkier build, a wider necktie will look better. In any case, don't buy a necktie wider than 4.5 inches (11.5 cm) as you don't want to go to extremes.

If you are shorter, you should avoid wide neckties, because they will make your body seem disproportionate. If you are very short, you might want to check out neckties that are both slimmer and shorter (less than 55 inches / 140 cm).

Remember that the more you move away from the 3 inch standard, the sooner it will go out of fashion. It will not be next year, but in a couple of years, the styles will most probably change.

In a good necktie collection, most of the neckties will be around the standard width, with a few on the skinnier or wider size depending on your build.

9. How to Match Neckties to an Outfit

Elegance is a subtle mix of originality and convention. It is not a science; many rules are bendable to a certain degree if you know how to pull off a particular style. It takes some instinct and practice. We men sometimes have problems with matching and coordinating different parts of our attire. Women usually do it better.

Matching neckties and shirts

Some people say that the way a man combines his shirts and neckties is the best way to find out how bold he is when it comes to fashion and how serious he takes his own style.

Matching neckties and shirts can be frustrating for many men especially because there are many possibilities regarding patterns and colors on both neckties and shirts. Of course, you can always stick to your usual solid colors combinations, but if you want to take your style to another level, then learning how to combine stripes, patterns and different colors is essential.

When you combine patterns, always pay attention to their color contrast, pattern similarity and their relative scale:

1. No matter how many patterns you wear, always repeat at least one color in all patterns. That color will be a connection that will link all these different patterns together. The best way to achieve the perfect combination is to determine the dominant color of your shirt, and then wear the necktie that has the same or similar color within its pattern.

2. If you are matching different patterns (for example stripes and dots), make sure that the sizes of the patterns are similar. The opposite is true if you are matching the same pattern on your shirt and your necktie (plus, don't forget point 3 that follows).

3. Always wear bigger and bolder patterns on your necktie and smaller on your shirt. Smaller surface of the necktie compared with larger surface of the shirt makes this combination much more pleasant for the eye than the other way around.

Solid with solid

Matching solid colored shirts and neckties is the easiest match to learn, so many men tend to stick with certain combinations for a long time. There's nothing wrong with a good solid with solid mix, but that doesn't mean that you always have to wear the same necktie with your favorite shirt. Instead of using contrast colors like most people do, try combining similar colors. For example, if you wear a light blue shirt, a solid dark blue necktie will look great on it. Another great way to change things a bit is to use some other fabric like wool or cotton for your necktie. Only be careful not to create too casual combination and then wear it to a formal occasion. Silk is still the most formal fabric when it comes to neckties, so use silk for work or weddings.

Solid and pattern

A great way to add something new to your style, and still keep it fairly simple and formal, is to mix solid with patterns. If you are a fan of patterned shirts, then a solid necktie will work perfectly with it. Make sure that the color of the necktie is from the same family as one of the colors on your shirt and it will work great. You'll have the same effect if you use a patterned necktie with a solid colored shirt. Again, pay attention to colors, and make sure that the color of your shirt is from the same family as one of the colors from the necktie pattern.

Pattern on pattern

These combinations are what most men avoid totally or get it completely wrong. Matching different patterns in your attire successfully is a clear sign that you are a man with style and knowledge to pull it off. Luckily you got this book to learn how to do it right.

There are many rules but also many exceptions. **Here are 7 universal, fundamental rules on how to achieve the perfect harmony and avoid a faux pas:**

1. Muted, darker tones make a more serious, respectful impression than bright colors and are the best choice for fall and winter wear. Brighter colors are better for casual or celebratory occasions and warm weather seasons.

2. Small motifs are more formal than large ones.

3. You CAN mix patterns BUT only if the patterns' scales are similar. The opposite is true if you are wearing the same pattern on a shirt and a necktie – they should be of different sizes, and not run in the opposite direction from each other.

4. Match a minor color from your necktie with a major color from your shirt or a major color from your necktie with a minor color from your shirt.

5. Never match your shirt and necktie in both color and pattern.

6. The width of your necktie should match the width of your suit jacket's lapels.

7. The materials of your necktie, shirt and jacket should be harmonized. Never combine heavy (wool) and light (linen), for example, or smooth (silk) with rough (wool). The softer the fabric of a necktie, the fancier and more formal it is. Do not combine fine silk neckties with rougher, textured fabrics such as wool, cotton, or linen.

Matching neckties and pocket squares

Have you ever tried wearing a pocket square, only to find yourself being the only one in the room with one? Maybe you enjoy being at the center of attention, but many men do not have the confidence to feel comfortable wearing a pocket square. Knowing how to wear one correctly will give you the élan to wear one more often and look great doing so!

When choosing which pocket square to wear, there is one rule that must be remembered:

Never ever wear the same color and pattern on the pocket square as on the necktie!

You can be more creative than that! Let the elements of the square pick up and/or contrast other elements of your outfit. This goes for the colors as well as the pattern and texture of the material.

Regarding color-coordination with pocket squares, the beauty is that there aren't many fixed rules. **You can wear it to complement anything in your outfit, be it the color on your shirt, necktie, or even socks.** When matching a pocket square to the color in your necktie, shirt or jacket, that color should be a minor or secondary color. Otherwise, the whole combination will become too matched, and that is not what we want. By the way, it is perfectly fine to wear a pocket square on the jacket without wearing a necktie.

The whole point of a pocket square is to create an interesting interplay between it and the rest of your outfit. As mentioned before, the match can be achieved either in color, pattern or texture.

In that sense, multicolored pocket squares are actually quite versatile and are nice to own as they can be worn with many colors. It is enough to pair only one color in the pocket square with anything else on your outfit.

For example, wearing a necktie or a shirt with red stripes can call for a pocket square containing some red (remember, some red, not completely or mostly red). It should not be of a matching pattern. In this example, dots or some other printed pattern would work well. Remember, if you have already achieved a match in color, avoid other matches (such as pattern or texture), because the whole combination will look almost academically assembled.

Ideally, you will want to let your neck area dominate, not your pocket square. That way, the eyes of others looking at you are drawn toward your face, not your breast pocket. The pocket square should complement your outfit, not dominate it or be too matchy or overly expressive.

A pocket square should ideally be a different material or texture than the necktie.. If your necktie is silk, a linen square will look the best; if your necktie is wool or cotton, silk in the breast pocket will add the proper textural balance.

10. Color Matching for Men 101

Gone are the days when certain colors were absolute no-nos in certain seasons. Today, anything goes if you know how to wear it!

Surely, for men, wearing color can be a tricky endeavor, but if you do it right, you will stand above the bland crowd and might attract some interesting encounters.

Tips for successful color matching for men

The best way to add color to your attire is through accessories (belts, neckties, pocket squares, socks). Colorful accessories make it possible to stay with safe colors (black or gray) for the majority of your outfit - your suit and shirt, while adding a splash of color to liven things up. This colorful detail will make a big difference.

One or two colorful pieces are enough to add 'pop' to an outfit. If you go for two, make sure they are in the same color family. Don't go for two bright colors, the second will only reduce the impact of the first piece.

Do not be cheap when shopping for colorful accessories. As they will stand out on you, you want them to be of the highest possible quality. People will notice the accessory! Spending extra for a higher quality piece will be money well spent.

If you want to wear a colored shirt or sweater and are afraid it might be too much for your style, try muting it by layering it under a blazer or a jacket.

The easiest way to match your necktie color with your shirt and jacket is to match the shirt to one of the necktie's colors, preferably a color that's dominant in the necktie and contrasts with the shirt. Alternatively, you can choose the necktie that has the greatest amount of the color you want to emphasize in your shirt and jacket.

You want to make sure your necktie stands out; do not let it blend in with the rest of the outfit.

Why are red neckties the most popular among politicians? Red color expresses confidence, power and passion, among other things. It is an image politicians want to transmit about themselves. They and their advisors know that a necktie can make or break someone's image! When chosen wisely, it brings color to a face, adds flair to a total appearance, and works as an accent to complete an outfit.

Different colors express and reflect a variety of characteristics and emotions. In the box on the next page are the most popular colors and their meanings. Remember that with neckties you can go much bolder in colors, since neckties should make a contrast with the rest of the outfit. Don't let your necktie blend with the rest of your outfit!

Your complexion and color matching

When choosing colors to wear, you need to be careful if you have dark or very fair skin. If you fall anywhere in the middle, don't worry - following the advices from this chapter so far will be enough.

If you have dark skin, hair and eyes, the colors you wear should contrast with your dark features. Try to go for white, pink, light blue or gray and avoid black, dark brown and navy blue.

If you have fair skin, blond or red hair, and a light eye color, your best match is to wear pastel colors which will blend in well with your skin tone. Try to go for light blue, brown, or beige and avoid red, pink, orange, yellow and purple. For the fairer-skinned, it is best to stay away from bright and vibrant colors.

What messages do you send with certain colors on your neckties?

Red color evokes dominance, power, confidence, but also passion and sexual energy. It makes great contrast with many of the safe colors, like gray, black or navy, so it is very versatile and worn often.

By wearing black necktie you transmit power, elegance and authority. It is a must for every man to have at least one black necktie in his wardrobe.

White necktie is worn in very formal settings and weddings. It shows an extremely clean appearance and higher social status.

Gray necktie is very neutral, specially worn with safe bet suit and shirt colors and therefore not making big contrast, but showing efficiency and class.

Depending on whether it is a dark blue / navy or light blue, it can convey different meanings. Dark blue and navy conveys strength and solidness, while light blue conveys friendliness.

Brown, especially dark brown shades convey earthy and masculine image.

Purple necktie gives a touch of royalty and exclusivity to your dress. It is a very popular color for neckties.

Pink necktie projects an upbeat attitude and good health. It is not any more considered as a feminine color and many men are embracing it into their outfits.

Yellow necktie conveys optimism, alertness and happiness. It does not look very good on pale skin men, so wear it carefully.

Burgundy necktie can be very classy as it conveys luxury, spirituality and extravagance.

11. How Not to Wear Neckties

Despite the fact that all you're really looking at is a small flap of material used to garnish an outfit, it's actually perfectly possible to make a thousand and one mistakes that subsequently take the sparkle off whatever look it was you were going for in the first place.

Here are the most common mistakes men make when wearing a necktie. All of them are a big no-no, so try to remember them next time when wearing a necktie.

#1: Badly tied neckties
One of the most common mistakes when it comes to neckties are the poorly tied ones. Mistakes may include a necktie tied too long or too short, flimsy-looking knot, a knot too big or too small, as well as knot that leaves you with the necktie's narrow end peeking out.

Your necktie must be tied appropriately in order for it to end near the center of your belt buckle. If you are extremely tall or short, buy neckties that are appropriate for you – longer ones for tall and shorter ones for short guys.

#2: Kitschy novelty neckties
Wearing novelty neckties definitely belongs to the list of mistakes. Novelty neckties are those kind of neckties that are deliberately kitschy and usually designed to make a statement. These include neckties featuring cartoon characters, commercial products or pop culture icons, and those made of unusual materials, such as plastic or wood. Don't wear those unless you are going to the carnival!

#3: Improper matching of colors, fabrics and patterns
This is much bigger topic that we discuss in previous chapters. If you are uncertain about a particular combination, rather simplify it than make this mistake. And as your knowledge grows, you will know how to match more complex combinations that will show that you know what you are doing.

#4: Stained or wrinkled neckties
Necktie is the primary focus point of your whole outfit, which means that if you have anything unsightly on your necktie, this will

be the first thing anyone sees and what your whole outfit is judged around.

Stained or wrinkled necktie should never be worn. Since neckties can't be washed and ironed like other clothes, it is a must that you untie your necktie after every wearing. You will increase the lifetime of your necktie by multifold by doing only this one thing! Also, after taking it off, hang your necktie on the rack to avoid it getting wrinkled. It can also be placed on a horizontal surface or rolled, but hanging is the best method as the force of gravity relaxes the fibers and decreases the wrinkles. More about it in the following chapters.

#5 Using clip-on neckties
Clip-ons are generally made for kids and having a grown man wearing a clip-on necktie sends very unserious message about the person wearing it.

#6 Wearing neckties on short sleeved shirts
Neckties should not be worn with short sleeved shirts. If you do, you are making a faux pas. If it is too hot outside, roll up your sleeves if you are wearing a necktie (that is ok in most cases) or leave a necktie at home when wearing a short sleeved shirt (maybe use a pocket square in your suit's jacket instead, to achieve more formal look).

12. Tie Bars and Tie Clips, Should You Wear Them?

Tie bars and tie clips are those accessories that you don't see very often on men and you might be wondering whether they are appropriate or not to wear.

Tie bars and tie clips first appeared in the 1920's, when neckties were increasing in popularity. Because of the delicate silky fabrics neckties were made of, men needed something to keep the necktie closer to the shirt and the whole look more uniformed. Even in the military, servicemen (and women!) were allowed to wear tie bars and clips as one of the few pieces of jewelry.

Still today, if worn correctly, they are quite trendy, but also can be very practical for the working professional. Keeping your necktie clean while moving around and about can be a challenge sometimes. These accessories can keep your shirt from looking disheveled and keep you looking sharp throughout the day.

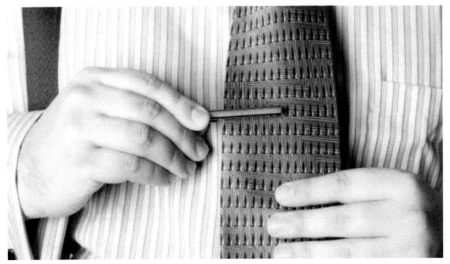

A tie clip

How to choose a tie bar / clip?

When it comes to picking tie bars and clips, usually three factors come into play:

1. The material on the inside of the clip, the part that meets the necktie, should be smooth in order not to snag any delicate fabric;

2. It should easily slide on, and not require any special tricks or tools to apply;

3. Lastly and most importantly, it shouldn't be heavy in weight. Nothing is more uncomfortable than feeling like a weight is hanging from your neck. Be aware of the pure gold tie bars and clips, as they may look stunning, but they are typically heavy and can cause some discomfort.

Tie bar and clip should be placed little bit above the middle of your necktie, typically between the third and fourth button of the dress shirt.

The width of the tie bar / clip should always be narrower than the necktie! Current trends are such that narrower tie bars / clips are more popular and are considered more modern, while wider ones are considered more conservative. So pick your width according to your necktie width and the whole combination you are wearing: skinny necktie and suit – narrower tie bar / clip; regular necktie and suit – wider tie bar / clip; but never as wide as the necktie.

Tie bar vs. tie clip

Tie bars and tie clips are actually very similar, and the difference is not that visible when wearing one as it is only the mechanism behind it that is different. Tie bars are made to slide onto the necktie and shirt connecting them and fastening the necktie into place, while tie clips usually come with a clasp and fasten both shirt and a necktie. They are both fashionable, both come in funky designs, and both are practical for men everywhere.

Whether it's a tie bar or a tie clip, they are perfect additions to an already classic look among men. When accessories are both fashionable and practical, that is a combination that's hard to resist!

13. Comfort in Summertime

If you are like most men, you probably don't like wearing a necktie in the summer. Sometimes, it is unavoidable - for work or a special event you have to wear one, although you would probably rather take off the suit and necktie altogether, and slip into shorts and short sleeves. And you are not the only one! There are so many men in the same position – feeling that their neckties are strangling them during those hot summer months.

How to dress for comfort in the summer heat

Even more important than in colder weather, your collar size should be chosen correctly. When you button the collar, it should not be too tight on your neck. You should be able to fit one finger between your shirt and your neck. That is just the right amount of space for comfort and proper fit.

When you knot your necktie, do not pull it too tight. If you see that your necktie falls too short after tying it, simply yanking it down will not fix the problem. You will need to untie it and start over, this time with more material falling on the longer end. When you get it right, the necktie will fall right to the belt buckle, and sit comfortably on the collar, looking good and not strangling you!

Another option is to tie the necktie with a looser knot style. The Trinity knot, for example, is not tied as tightly as other knots; it also has a unique and stunning look that is sure to start a conversation. The Trinity knot works well with solid color neckties or neckties with a small pattern. For maximum impact, tie the Trinity on a diagonally striped necktie: tied one direction it will create a pinwheel pattern at the knot, and tied the other direction it will create a triangle. The Trinity takes some practice to learn, but there are great videos on *YouTube* that demystify the process.

In summer, you should opt for lighter materials, like linen or cotton, especially for the suit and shirt. These materials are great for summer months; they wick away moisture and sweat due to their weave and light weight. When choosing a necktie to accompany a linen or cotton suit, opt for the same lightweight materials, or wear silk which is universal. Definitely leave wool neckties for the winter!

Also in the summer, choose colors that hide sweat well. All men sweat, especially in the armpits and around the belly. If you choose colors that hide it well, like white, yellow or pink as opposed to blue, for example, you will feel more confident in yourself.

Even if you are very tempted to wear a necktie with short sleeved shirt, don't do it unless you are not worried about breaking basic dressing principles.

„Neckties do not go on short sleeved shirts!"

Finally, **if you can avoid the necktie, but still want to look elegant, wear a pocket square instead.** That will maintain your formal appearance, and relieve your neck from being constrained. The pocket square definitely works for more casual events, and you might even get away with it at work, provided your company does not have a draconian necktie policy. Try it, and see what the reaction is. Not many men wear pocket squares, and you will be noticed for your smart styling sense.

14. What to Wear to a Job Interview?

Job interviews are tricky because the dress code can vary greatly depending on the type of company and position you are applying for. If you are interviewing for a corporate job in law or the financial sector, you will dress much more conservatively than if you are applying for a creative position in the entertainment industry.

The basic rule is that you should dress for the interview as you would for a day at the office. That way you make it clear that you understand the nature of the business.

But how do you know the office dress code? Do your homework before showing up for the interview - research the company online or ask friends and acquaintances who work in similar fields.

When in doubt, it is better to over-dress rather than under-dress. It is much easier to dress down while in the waiting room – by removing your necktie or a suit jacket for example – than it is to style up if you are too casual. Also, making sure you feel comfortable in what you are wearing will help you remain relaxed and confident.

As for necktie choice, silk is usually the best material. Wool, linen and cotton neckties are probably too casual.

Some basic tips to keep in mind

- Your safest bet is to stick with solid colors, darker tones and clean lines.
- Wearing the right size is essential. Your clothes should conform to your body. If any garment is too tight or too loose, it will ruin the look and you will not feel comfortable.
- All clothes in the outfit should be well laundered and ironed.
- Your belt and shoes should always match, same with your pants and socks.
- Clean shaven or neatly trimmed facial hair is essential.

Good luck on nailing that interview and getting the job you deserve!

Caring for Neckties

15. Necktie Crimes

We are all guilty of doing things we shouldn't. And although we know we shouldn't, we still do. In many cases though, men simply do not know how to care for their neckties.

Here are things you should never ever do with a necktie:

1. Do not leave it tied after you've taken it off. Untie it every time.

2. Do not wear the same necktie on two consecutive days. Apart from giving the impression that it is your only necktie, it will fatigue the necktie by not giving it time to regain its shape and minimize wrinkles.

3. Do not tuck your necktie into anything! Not into your waistband, not behind the belt buckle, and not in the gap between the shirt buttons. In the car, put the seat belt under your necktie, not over it.

4. Do not toss your necktie behind your neck, for example when eating.

5. Do not loosen your necktie unless you are in the process of taking it off completely.

6. Do not wash your necktie - take it to a good dry cleaner.

7. Do not iron your necktie - if there are wrinkles, use only steam to get creases out.

Stick with these rules and you will considerably extend the lifetimes of your neckties!

16. How to Clean Neckties

To most men, cleaning a necktie is much more an afterthought than cleaning a clothing item such as a suit or a shirt which you must dry-clean and iron regularly. Nevertheless, if you spend a bit more on a high quality necktie, with proper care, it can last a lifetime!

Of course, the first step in ensuring that your necktie has a long life is investing in one that is well made. How to buy a quality necktie has been covered in Chapter 3.

To prolong the lifetime of a silk necktie, you should never knot it too tight, and even more importantly, it must be fully and carefully unknotted after wearing (using the exact opposite order of the steps used to tie it), and then stored, preferably hung. The force of gravity relaxes the fibers and decreases the wrinkles. That is the reason you should not wear the same necktie for two days in a row – a necktie should be given a rest, to get back into its normal, stretched position.

If you get a stain on your necktie, unfortunately you can't wash it in the machine, or by hand, as this will ruin it. A necktie consists of layers of different fabrics which, when washed, will not shrink the same way, and the necktie's shape will be destroyed. A high quality dry cleaner is the only option for stain removal. Don't try to use commercially available stain removers - you might make things worse.

If your necktie gets wrinkled to the point that hanging in the closet will not fix it, try this: hang your necktie in a steamy bathroom (after showering, for example) for half an hour, and then lay it flat to dry.

To maintain a necktie's full color and prevent fading, always store it in a dark closet or a drawer.

When traveling, use a necktie case (preferably leather) in which the necktie lays flat, or simply roll the necktie and place it into a (clean) shoe or inside a shirt's collar.

As you can see, keeping a necktie in great shape requires adhering to just a few simple rules!

Tying Neckties

17. Tie with Confidence! The Only 3 Knots You Need to Know

There is no getting around it, if you are going to wear neckties, you have to know how to knot them. This knowledge is part of men's culture. Thinking that you can get away with asking someone to tie it and then keeping it tied in your closet is not acceptable!

To recycle the old saying: Learning to knot a necktie is like learning to ride a bicycle; it takes practice, but once you learn it, you will never forget.

There are about 85 ways to tie a necktie, but there are just three basic knots you need in your catalogue. Which one you use will depend mainly on the collar of your shirt, and in some cases the length of your necktie and your build.

Three most popular necktie knots: Windsor, Half-Windsor and 'Four in hand'

The most popular necktie knots, from biggest to smallest

Windsor

This is named for England's Duke of Windsor. It is sometimes also called a Full Windsor. It is the most traditional necktie knot. The Windsor knot is the only knot that is to be used by Royal Air Force personnel in the UK when wearing their black necktie while in uniform, and by personnel in any branch of the Canadian Armed Forces.

Characteristics of the Windsor knot are:

• A bigger, symmetrical, well-balanced knot - therefore the Windsor goes well only with wide, spread-collar shirts.

• It takes some practice to tie well.

• The Windsor uses more of the material, so it is good for longer neckties and/or shorter men.

• When tied correctly the knot is tight and does not slip away from the collar during wear, therefore it's very trouble-free to wear.

• A Windsor knot best compliments a strong square or round face, or a face with facial hair due to its size. This provides balance with the wearer's face.

How to tie the Windsor knot:

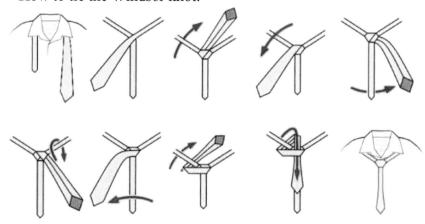

Half-Windsor

Although called the Half-Windsor, it is actually about 75% the size of the Windsor knot.

Characteristics of the Half-Windsor knot are:

• It will make a medium (lightweight necktie) to large (heavier necktie) knot.

• It has a symmetrical look.

• It's versatile: the Half-Windsor looks good with any face shape and with almost any type of shirt.

How to tie the Half-Windsor knot:

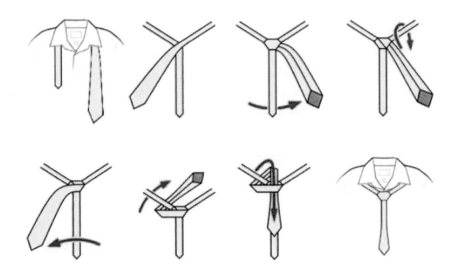

'Four in Hand'

The 'Four in Hand' necktie knot is the most popular and if you only know one knot, it is probably this one. It is also the easiest one to do.

Characteristics of the 'Four in Hand' knot are:

- A small, tidy, slightly asymmetrical triangular knot.
- It looks best with narrow shirt collars.
- It is easy to tie.
- It uses the least of the necktie's length, therefore is good for shorter neckties and/or taller men.

How to tie 'Four in Hand' knot:

Mark Davids

Bow Ties

A Practical Guide

2015 edition

1. Are Bow Ties Coming Back?

Often associated with servers, tutors and nerds, the bow tie is no longer the bastion of these stereotypes. Lately, many men have discovered that a bow tie can be a reputable fashion accessory, able to balance their outfits and improve their appearance.

Pre-tied silk bow tie

Spotting a guy in a bow tie is still quite an unusual experience, but bow ties do seem to be coming back into fashion. Lately, many TV shows have been promoting neckties and bow ties to youngsters as a cool fashion statement. Hopefully, in the near future, a man with a bow tie will not be a rare sight.

Wearing a bow tie today will mark you as a strong individual, a person of style who is not afraid to be different. If the trend continues in favor of bow ties, you might also be recognized as a trendsetter. Not such a bad reputation, right? So, if you are not afraid of being at the center of attention, perhaps you should adopt the practice of wearing a bow tie.

Bow ties for men descended from the cravat. They came onto the scene around the end of the 19th century, when for practical reasons, much smaller men's ties were required. Since its birth, the bow tie has existed in many forms and sizes: floppy, stiff, geometric, bigger, smaller, etc. It wasn't until the beginning of the 20th century when the bow tie we know today took prominence.

The bow tie craze – is it a fad or the start of a long-term trend?

Everyone is talking about bow ties lately – from fashion blogs, to social media such as Twitter and Tumblr to some of the most popular TV shows – *Glee* and *Doctor Who* possibly the most influential of these.

But, is it just another temporary fad or will the bow tie trend stick around for a long time? In other words, should you stock up on bow ties or just let it pass?

First, let's see some proof that bow ties are indeed becoming increasingly popular. If you head to Google trends and research the popularity of 'bow ties' as a search term on Google, the last several years will show this trend line:

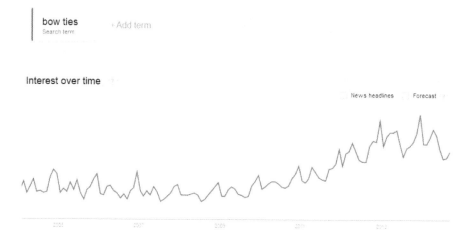

You can see the increase since 2009, and the even greater rise in popularity since mid-2011.

If you use the same tool to compare the popularity of bow ties to neckties, a surprising trend emerges:

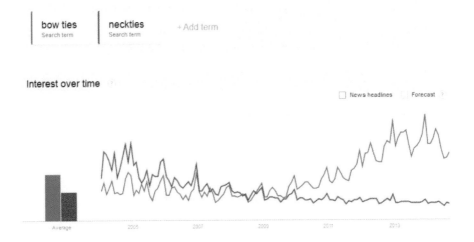

The blue line represents the number of Google searches for 'bow ties' while the red line represents those for 'neckties'. Indeed, bow ties are now more commonly searched for than neckties.

Of course, this only represents Google internet searches since 2005, but the internet is omnipresent in our lives today and our online behavior increasingly represents our real lives with great accuracy. What we search for and read about online, and the things we like and share on Facebook and other social media platforms usually mirror what we like and consume in our real lives! And, as seen above, we have been searching more frequently about bow ties for some years now.

Fans of '*Doctor Who*' know that bow ties are cool thanks to the '*11th Doctor.*' *The Telegraph* reports that in the month after the episode 'The Eleventh Hour' aired, bow tie sales at one UK menswear store exploded by 94%. *ThinkGeek.com* also quickly sold out their 'Bow Ties Are Cool' T-shirts.

'Doctor Who' says bow ties are cool!

Both neckties and bow ties developed over the centuries through many different styles and sizes, but somehow neckties have always been more popular. A driving factor for this is because they have been adopted by the mainstream business world. Bow ties have been reserved for either formal or celebratory events ('black-tie' and 'white-tie' events), or for certain professions where the bow tie is more practical, like medicine and dentistry or the food-service industry. Additionally, artists, bohemians and people with a strong sense of style seem drawn to bow ties.

This time around however, it seems that bow ties have strong winds blowing in their favor to become mainstream fashion accessories for men and compete neck to neck, if you will, with neckties.

2. Types of Bow Ties

Bow ties come in **three forms**:
- Bow ties that must be tied,
- Pre-tied bow ties, and
- Clip-on style bow ties.

The most popular bow ties today are pre-tied. They are practical, flexible and when worn, they look like good, old-fashioned bow ties you have to tie yourself. Pre-tied bow ties are available in many sizes, materials and patterns. Luckily, they are very easy to wear as there is no tying required.

Pre-tied bow tie

Having a bow tie you tie yourself however, will set you apart as a gentleman of substance and style. It is a skill you should learn, as it tells the world you are concerned enough about your appearance to put some effort into it.

Although tying a bow tie is not as complex as it seems, many people avoid it completely and opt for pre-tied bow ties. But if you really want to learn how to tie a bow tie, stay tuned as we will discuss this later in the book. If you prefer a more hands-on education, go to any menswear store that sells them and ask a sales person to teach you how to tie one. Unlike with neckties, there is only one bow tie knot.

Self-tied bow ties

Clip-on ties just clip on to your shirt's collar and do not go around your neck. They are not very classy; many stylists and designers have dismissed them as a novelty. If you really do not want to have to tie your own bow tie, at least opt for a pre-tied tie. It cannot be stated enough: **clip-on ties are tacky, avoid them entirely!**

Clip-on bow ties

Styles of proper bow ties

Bow ties come in different **styles and sizes**. The following are the most common bow tie styles:

Butterfly Bow Tie
The butterfly is the largest of the bow ties. The wings of the bow are between 3" and 3.5" and are reminiscent of butterfly wings. Some consider these larger bow ties slightly less formal, but they look good on men that have a larger neck size and bigger face and chin.

Butterfly bow tie

Semi-Butterfly Bow Tie (Thistle or Classic Bow Tie)
This type of bow tie has a wing size of 2.25" to 2.75". It is the most common bow tie size worn at black tie functions, and chances are that if you own bow ties, they are mostly this size. This style is a safe choice for any black-tie function regardless of the wearer's height and weight.

Semi-butterfly bow tie

Batwing Bow Tie (Narrow Bow Tie)

The batwing is a narrower bow tie with a wing size measuring 1.5" to 2" wide. It looks best on slimmer men with a narrow neck/collar. This type of bow tie is considered slightly less formal, but can still be worn at black tie functions.

Batwing bow tie

Pointed Bow Ties

Bow ties with pointed wings are available in any of the three sizes mentioned above. They are perfect for those that want something unique while still adhering to a strict black-tie dress code.

Bow tie with pointed wings

3. Where and How to Buy Bow Ties

Bow ties can be bought in many shops, offline or online. The benefits of buying bow ties in brick-and-mortar stores are that you can try the bow tie on and get some advice from the sales personnel. Online however, you can easily shop around, compare prices and look at many different styles and designs in just a couple of minutes, all from your sofa or office. If you know your size, buying your bow tie online can be less expensive as well, as there are many good online shops competing for your attention and trust.

That said; if you want to visit some offline stores to see their offerings, don't miss Brooks Brothers, Macy's, Nordstrom, Barneys and other similar retailers selling men's clothing. You might check their websites as well.

There are many online retailers specializing in ties that offer ties of excellent quality. Very often their bow ties are made in limited quantities; therefore, you know you are buying exclusive products, often for a very affordable price.

Some recommended online bow tie retailers are:

http://www.dolbeau.ca/ - Canadian brand making exquisite neckties and bow ties with unique materials, all by hand. All their editions are very small and when sold out, they are gone.

http://www.generalknot.com/ - Neckties and bow ties, handmade in the USA with vintage fabrics. Every product comes with an exclusively numbered card, which means your bow tie will be a really unique piece!

http://www.bergbergstore.com/ - Norwegian brand making bow ties (and other accessories for men) designed in Norway and hand made in Italy. Often they have very interesting designs.

http://www.drakes-london.com/ - founded in 1977, today Drakes is the largest independent producer of bow ties and neckties hand-made in England, offering also a wide range of shirts and pocket squares.

http://www.asuitablewardrobe.net/ - the clothing site for stylish men, combining award-winning editorial content with hand-made clothing and accessories from dozens of makers like Simonnot-Godard of France, Drake's London and Neapolitan makers. Like the great haberdashers of years past, it stocks products, such as braces, bow ties and socks, in a wider range of sizes than is common elsewhere in the world, including made to measure versions of some items.

http://www.bensilver.com/ - offers classic, refined and tasteful clothing and accessories for gentlemen who enjoy the added dash of updated color. They present fresh collections of fine neckwear every season.

http://pierreponthicks.com/ - Mac and Katherine McMillan launched Pierrepont Hicks in 2009 out of a desire to make the perfect tie. In the meantime they have launched more products each season, including outerwear for both men and women, always remaining focused on accessories for life's travels, adventures and celebrations.

http://www.thetiebar.com/ - "Smart, stylish ties don't have to cost a fortune" – that's their motto. The Tie Bar offers vast selection of colorful and stylish pieces of men's accessories at extremely low prices (silk bow ties for as low as $15!).

http://www.etsy.com – a marketplace for many independent designers. Search their site for bow ties and discover some great bow ties made by designers from all over the world!

When shopping for high quality bow ties, go for natural materials (silk, wool, cotton) and make sure that the bow tie is well crafted and well-stitched together. The people behind these websites are very knowledgeable about the origins of their products and would be happy to answer any of your questions. Look for a contact email and don't hesitate to email them with your inquiries.

When shopping online for a bow tie, pay close attention to its size. Although most bow ties offered today come in standard sizes, you don't want to be surprised by a bow tie that shows up and is too large or too small. The right bow tie should not be broader than your neck, and when worn, its ends should not extend past the tips of your shirt's collar nor the width of your eyes!

Wearing cheap bow ties can hurt your reputation

People today associate themselves with their favorite consumer brands and are very sensitive to the image they are projecting to the world around them. In the world of menswear, wearing cheap ties can ruin your style, and even your reputation. Wearing bow ties shows that you are a man of style, and wearing something cheap will only destroy that perception. Wearing a tie is a cultural symbol, a sign of respect. Wearing a cheap tie ruins that symbolism. Better to eschew the tie altogether, than to wear a lackluster bow tie!

The good news is that bow ties are generally less expensive than regular neckties. Even better news is that they are more often on sale. Look for nice bow ties when stores are having their seasonal sales.

How many bow ties do you need?

If you attend formal events where the expected attire is 'black-tie' or 'white-tie,' you will need at least one black bow tie and one white bow tie. For other colors or patterns, it depends on your wardrobe and whether you will wear them formally or in more casual occasions.

4. Wearing Bow Ties - What's IN Now?

The time for bow ties has come, that we already confirmed. But what is 'IN' now? What are the current trends? Here are some tips for wearing bow ties now:

Mix Patterns
Don't be afraid to combine patterns when you've chosen to add bow ties to your look. Small polka dots and thin stripes go well together, and thicker stripes and paisley are a winning match. Since this pattern mix will give your outfit a lot of character, be careful with colors and have at least one color repeating in both patterns.

Go For Texture
While most formal bow ties are made of silk, you don't have to choose this dressy material every time you are wearing a bow tie. Wool bow ties are particularly eye-catching with cotton shirts, and cotton or even denim bow ties look great if you're going to a casual event. In cold weather, you may want to finish off your textured look with a tweed sport coat or a vest. The point is to mix different materials and textures together.

Slim It Down
Large bow ties were all the rage a few years ago, but those days are long gone. Slim bow tie is your best bet for staying stylish and chic, regardless of the season. Slim bow ties also look neat and refined even if you're wearing one in casual fabric. It looks great with anything from a tailored suit or tuxedo to a preppy look that includes a cardigan and yacht shorts.

Go Casual
Keep in mind that bow ties are not just for weddings and galas anymore. You can wear a bow tie with virtually any outfit, as long as you pair it with a collared shirt. For example, jean shirts pair well with plaid bow ties. If you have a patterned sport coat or blazer, wearing a solid-colored bow tie in the same material completes the look handsomely.

5. Where to Wear Bow Ties?

If you want to express your individuality in the style of Abraham Lincoln, Winston Churchill, Frank Sinatra or Oscar Wilde, you know what you need to do. They were all known for their loyalty to bow ties!

Winston Churchill wearing his famous bow tie

Any social function, regardless of its formality, is meant to be entertaining and fun. But for many people, an invitation to a corporate, charity or celebratory event can be a source of frustration because they are unsure of how to dress.

Social considerations like these can be dealt with in a calm and logical manner. It is not rocket science and you do not need any special credentials to enjoy the party! So, calm down and follow carefully.

What should you wear to a party?

This is probably the most important thing to get right. Dressing appropriately will make you feel confident and relaxed. Dressing inappropriately will make you spend the entire evening planning your escape.

Look at the invitation; it usually says what the dress code is. If not, call the host and ask about expected attire. If this makes you nervous, just remember: you do not want to be the one getting it wrong.

Let's cover many common dress codes, from least to most formal:

Casual – depends on the season; in the summer it means shorts and a polo shirt and in winter, jeans and a sweater

Casual Chic – a sports coat or sweater and slacks

Business Casual – a shirt without a tie and a sports jacket

Festive Informal – a suit and a brightly colored tie

Cocktail Attire – a dark suit or dressy sports coat

Business Attire – a suit and a tie

Semiformal – a dark suit and a tie

Black Tie Optional – a tuxedo or a dark suit with a tie

Black Tie – a tuxedo, black cummerbund or vest, white shirt, cuff links, black bow tie and polished black shoes.

White Tie – black tails, white waistcoat, white shirt with wing collars and white bow tie.

In any case, if you are not completely sure, it is always better to be slightly over-dressed than under-dressed.

As you can see, a bow tie is obligatory only if you are going to a 'black-tie' or a 'white-tie' event. In that case you will be wearing it with a tuxedo. By definition, a tuxedo is a complete outfit that includes a jacket, trousers (usually with a silk stripe down the side), a bow tie, and often, a cummerbund or a vest.

A tuxedo (Also notice the pocket square - a very classy touch)

Depending on whether the type of the event you are attending is 'black-tie' or 'white-tie', you should wear either a black or white bow tie with a tux. No other colors are advisable.

The last alternative to a black tux is a classic black suit. If worn with a straight collar white shirt and solid, black tie (necktie or a bow tie), it can be an acceptable, although not preferable, alternative to a tuxedo. Opt for a true tuxedo if you want to show yourself in your best light.

The 'black-tie' dress code is meant to act just as that - a dress code. The objective of 'black-tie' is to dress appropriately, not to be a trendsetter. If you stand out from the crowd, you are doing something wrong.

In all other cases you can choose to wear a bow tie or not. Although bow ties are normally considered formal menswear, they can be (and increasingly are) also worn in more casual environments. They are a versatile accessory, easily worn with or without a coat, with slacks or with jeans and a leather jacket.

How to Rock Bow Ties at Weddings

If you have been invited to a wedding or will be the groom at this very special occasion, you may have considered wearing a bow tie. There are a number of ways to wear a bow tie to a wedding depending on the event's level of formality. Here are a few helpful tips.

Formal Weddings

A formal wedding is the ideal opportunity to wear a bow tie (remember the 'Black-Tie' and 'White-Tie' dress code?). If you are the groom, a silk black or white bow tie is a must. Such bow tie pairs well with a tuxedo. As a groomsman, go with the groom's wishes when choosing the color of your bow tie. Or, for instance, you may wear a bow tie that features one of the wedding colors. Another possibility is - if the groom wears white bow tie, wear a black one, and vice versa.

Semi-Formal Weddings

If you'll be a guest at the semi-formal wedding, think about how you would dress for the job if you worked in a business setting. A well-fitting suit and black shoes are appropriate for attending the nuptials. If you choose a solid-color black or navy suit, a bow tie in a subtle pattern in contrast color will help you stand out without drawing too much attention to yourself. Thin stripes or paisley make dashing patterns for your bow tie and look great against a crisp white button-down shirt.

Evening Weddings

A wedding that takes place in the evening, but isn't formal, should put you in the mind of going on a first date. You should look dressy but not too stuffy. A bow tie in a striking color that goes well with your shirt is ideal. Bow ties in various materials like tweed, cotton or even leather, are also attractive and show off your daring sense of style. If the wedding is during the spring or summer, you may want to go with a vest instead of a sport coat to complete the look.

Just like the bride and bridesmaids will want to try on their dresses and accessories before the wedding, you'll need to do the same with your bow tie. Make sure the collar of the shirt you're wearing fits around the bow tie properly, and make sure the tie isn't too large or too small. Most of all, wear your bow tie with confidence, and you'll likely be complimented on how attractive you look.

What about the office - are bow ties appropriate in the professional arena?

Whether bow ties are professional enough to be worn in the office will depend mainly on two factors – where you live and which industry you work in.

In some countries, it is normal to see men wearing bow ties in the office; in some, the regular necktie is more appropriate and wearing a bow tie will give you a reputation of eccentricity. In the US, bow ties are generally more accepted in the South than in the North.

Another factor is the industry you work in and the corporate culture of the company you work for. If you work in a creative environment, such as an advertising firm, fashion house, or in publishing, a bow tie may be accepted and even viewed as trendy. Even some law firms consider bow ties very traditional and respectful. On the other hand, the financial industry would be one where bow ties are very rare and you would have hard time blending in. In any case, observe how managers and executives in your company dress - you should generally follow their lead.

All things considered, after you have incorporated bow ties into your wardrobe, there's no reason why they cannot become the perfect day-to-day accessories. They will give you an air of individuality and creativity; who knows, you could become the go-to guy in your circles for fashion advice.

6. Color Matching your Bow Tie – How to Do it Right

Many men find color-coordination of their clothes difficult; fortunately in many cases, they are aware of it. Therefore you will often see very safe, if somewhat boring, color choices like black, gray, navy and white. These are the easiest to match and you can hardly go wrong with them as they are quite universal.

Gone are the days when certain colors were frowned upon in certain seasons. Today, anything goes if you know how to wear it properly!

Surely, for men, wearing color can be a tricky endeavor, but if you do it right, you will stand above the crowd! Men throughout history have attracted the attention of potential employers, clients, and even lovers by having a great sense of style.

Tips for successful color matching

The best way to add color to your attire is through accessories (belts, ties, pocket squares, socks). By adding the visual spark through accessories, you add interest to your whole outfit, even if all the other colors worn are safe bets, like black or gray. This colorful detail will make a big difference. Bow ties are perfect for adding a splash of color to your outfit.

Try to go for only one or two colorful pieces per outfit. If choose to wear two, make sure they are in the same color family. Don't choose two bright colors. The second will not add anything; it will only reduce the impact of the first piece.

Do not be cheap when shopping for colorful accessories. As they will stand out on you, you want them to be of the highest quality possible. People will notice these pieces, no doubt about that! It will be money well spent.

The easiest way to match the color of your bow tie with those of your shirt and jacket is to match the shirt to one of the bow tie's colors, preferably one that's dominant in the bow tie and contrasts with the shirt. Another option is to choose the bow tie that has the greatest amount of the color you want to emphasize in your shirt and jacket. You will want to make sure your bow tie stands out, so make sure it doesn't blend in with the rest of the outfit.

Author Mark Davids

Color matching your complexion

When choosing colors to wear, you need to be careful if you have dark or very pale skin. If you fall the middle of this spectrum, don't worry: follow the advice above and you will look great!

If you have dark skin, hair and eyes, the colors you wear should contrast with your dark features. Opt for white, pink, light blue, gray and avoid black, dark brown and navy blue.

If you have pale skin with blond or red hair and fair eyes, your best match is to wear pastel colors which will match well with your skin tone. Look for garments that are light blue, brown or beige and avoid red, pink, orange, yellow, purple. Generally avoid bright and vibrant colors.

What messages do you send with certain colors?

What is the meaning of certain colors? What energy and subliminal messages do you send when wearing them? Here are some basic meanings:

Red – dominance, power, confidence, attention, sexual energy
Black – elegance, authority, power, confidence
White – virtue, cleanliness
Gray – class, efficiency
Blue – trustworthiness, seriousness, intellect, calmness
Burgundy – passion, spirituality, extravagance
Pink – upbeat attitude, health
Yellow – alertness, optimism

7. How to Match Bow Ties to Suits and Shirts

If you've decided to add bow ties to your wardrobe, there are lots of stylish ways to incorporate this accessory into your suits and dress shirt options. Here are a few tips to keep in mind when you're pairing your bow tie with a suit or shirt so you can express your personal style and look your best.

Pair Your Patterns Wisely
Remember not to be too *cliche* with the patterns when it comes to wearing a suit or a shirt with a bow tie. If your suit/shirt is pinstriped, a bow tie in the same pattern will look too costume-y. Instead, try a bow tie with, for example, paisley pattern. This combination is both classy and edgy. Only one tip: when you want to wear a patterned bow tie and a patterned shirt together (different patterns on each), make sure the patterns are similar in size.

Of course, you can also contrast the pattern of the suit/shirt by wearing a solid-colored bow tie. Choose a bow tie that is of minor, and possible brighter, color on your suit/shirt. For instance, if the stripes are gray and blue, opt for the blue bow tie.

Use the Color Wheel

When you're matching your bow tie with your suit/shirt, don't be afraid of color. A tie in a vivid hue can wake up a black or navy blue suit and add just the right amount of character and can make your attire a little more original.

It's a good idea to consult the color wheel when you're matching your suit, shirt and bow tie. If your suit is gray, which is considered a "cool" color, a blue or purple dress shirt will look great with the suit and make it more interesting. A bow tie that is slightly darker than your dress shirt makes your look classy.

Keep in mind that colors on the opposite side of the color wheel work well together as well. Red (a warm color) and green (a cool color) look great together, as do orange and blue. So, if you're wearing a suit in a neutral color, a shirt that represents one side of the color wheel and a bow tie that showcases a hue on the opposing side of the wheel will make your outfit particularly striking. A dark gray suit with a burgundy dress shirt and hunter green tie is fitting for a fall or winter occasion. A light blue dress shirt and bow tie in a subtle orange hue is a winning combination if you're heading to a spring or summer event.

Mix and Match Materials

Pairing different materials together will make your outfit especially interesting and visually appealing. For instance, a silk bow tie with a dress shirt made from quality cotton is always a winning combination no matter what type of dressy event you're attending. If you're going for a more casual feel, a cotton bow tie matched with a shirt in similar material is appropriate. Other casual materials like tweed and wool also look great with cotton shirts.

Size Matters

Finally, remember that size is important when you're choosing a bow tie. The wider your vest or sport coat is, the larger your bow tie can be. If your suit jacket is fitted, a slim bow tie is best. Your bow tie should extend slightly past both sides of your chin, but shouldn't be large enough to line up with your ears. When your bow tie measurements are in line with your outerwear, this makes for a streamlined look that gives you a great silhouette.

8. Matching Bow Ties with Pocket Squares and Suspenders

Bow Ties and Pocket Squares

Bow ties and pocket squares complement each other quite nicely. There are just couple rules to keep in mind.

First of all, when dressing for a 'black-tie' event, the bow tie should be solid black, while for a 'white-tie' event, the bow tie should be white. In both cases, the pocket square should be bright white or cream to match the shirt color and to set contrast to the jacket. In the rare case you are wearing a white tuxedo, the pocket square should be black.

Another rule is that you should never match a pocket square exactly to the bow tie in color and pattern. What is important is that the colors of both bow tie and pocket square harmonize with the rest of the outfit.

With pocket squares, the beauty is that there aren't many fixed rules; you can wear it to match anything in your outfit, your shirt or tie, even your socks. The whole point of a pocket square is the interesting interplay between it and the rest of your outfit, even if it is just to contrast all the other colors you are wearing. The match can be achieved either in color, pattern or material.

Bow Ties and Suspenders

Suspenders may be worn with or without a necktie or bow tie, but if worn with any style of tie, they should both match the shade of the shoes. Suspenders should sit comfortably over the shoulders and reach down to the pant level in the front and back without too much adjustment. Suspenders are to be worn without a belt! Traditional suspenders have two holes at the end of each strap, front and back, which attach to small buttons on the inside of the pants waistline. If your trousers does not have these, ask a tailor to add them for you.

Another thing is – keep things in proportion. Slim bow tie (like Batwing bow tie) looks better when paired with thin suspenders, and wider bow tie (like Butterfly and Semi-Butterfly bow tie) with wider suspenders. Keeping this rule in mind will give your body more proportion and balance.

Bow tie and suspenders

9. How to Tie a Bow Tie - Step by Step

Although you can get pre-tied bow ties in many shops, the greatest coolness factor is achieved if you get a real, self-tied bow tie that you actually tie. After you learn it, you will never go back to pre-tied bow ties.

Luckily there is only one way of doing it, so there is only one knot to learn.

How to tie a bow tie?

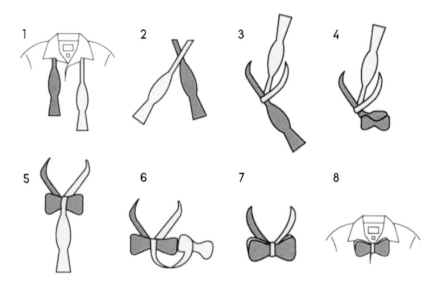

How to tie a bow tie. Source: Tieatieeasily.com

Step 1

Place the bow tie around your neck so one end of the bow tie will be slightly longer than the other (about 2 inches).

Step 2

Bring the longer end of the bow tie across the shorter end, above it, to the other side.

Step 3

Pass the long end of the bow tie inside the loop around your neck, upwards. Tighten the knot around your neck as it will be difficult to tighten it later on. This is the base knot.

Step 4

Fold the short end of the bow tie to form a bow shape. Place the bow directly above the base knot.

Step 5

Turn the long end of the bow tie downwards, above the folded bow shape.

Step 6

Fold the long end of the bow tie to a bow shape (just like you did with the short end in step 4).

Step 7

Insert the bow-shaped long end into the hole behind the bow-shaped short end (the hole is between the base knot and the back of the short end bow). Insert the long end through this hole, up to the middle of the bow (the narrow section).

Step 8

Tighten the bow tie by holding both ends. Adjust the bow tie to get a symmetrical and even form in both sides.

These eight steps are all that are required to tie the perfect bow tie. If it is not perfect, keep practicing. You will soon have it memorized and perfected!

Mark Davids

Pocket Squares for Men

The Complete Guide

2015 edition

1. What are Pocket Squares?

If you are reading this book, you probably already know what pocket squares are, but just to be sure, let's first define what they are and what they are not.

„Pocket squares are small squares of fabric made especially for suit or blazer breast pockets.“

They should not, by any means, be confused with handkerchiefs. **Pocket squares are for decorative use only.** Do not use it to wipe your nose, nor lend it to someone else for that purpose. That is what regular cotton or paper handkerchiefs are for, and they should be kept in your pants pocket.

James Bond always looks sharp with a pocket square in his breast pocket.

Origins of the pocket square date back to the ancient Greeks, when the wealthy would carry perfumed handkerchiefs. Throughout history, English and French noblemen also possessed perfumed and embroidered hankies to protect their sense of smell from the stench of dirty streets and the not so worthy.

The pocket square was originally kept in the pocket of pants because it was not very hygienic to keep putting a dirty cloth into the breast pocket of a jacket or shirt. This changed by the 19th century when two-piece suits became fashionable and many men started putting the pocket square into the breast pocket. By the early 20th century the pocket square was quickly becoming strictly a fashion accessory. Men would typically carry 2 handkerchiefs, one to act as a cloth, which would be kept in the pants pocket and the other to act as a pocket square, which was kept in the breast pocket.

Over the years, due to the growth of mainstream paper handkerchiefs such as Kleenex, alongside medical studies claiming that handkerchiefs were unhygienic, and transforming fashion trends, handkerchiefs made of fabric became a rare thing to see a man carrying. On the other hand, pocket squares became less functional and more fashionable, developing into a category of male jewelry.

Size and materials of pocket squares

There are many different sizes of pocket squares on the market, ranging mainly from 10 to 18 inches per side, but there is no one ideal pocket square size. Choosing the right pocket square size is directly linked to knowing the material it is made of.

„Usually, thicker fabrics (linen, cotton) tend to be better in smaller squares, while fine and light fabrics such as silk are made in bigger sizes."

If the pocket square is too big, it might become too bulky when folded and therefore will make your pocket look bumpy. On the other hand, if the square is too small, it might move around or fall inside your pocket, distorting its shape and fold. Therefore, weight of the cloth needs to be taken into consideration when judging whether pocket square is too big or too small.

As already noted, pocket squares can be made of several different types of fabrics, or their blends, but most of them made either from cotton, linen, silk or polyester.

- Linen and cotton pocket squares can come in smaller sizes, as small as 10 inches per side if their fabric is sturdier. They can go up to 16 inches per side for lighter fabrics. They can be ironed (to get a sharper look), so they can make a really nice TV fold as well as any of the point folds. Linen and cotton pocket squares look much better on a fine wool suit jacket than on rougher fabrics like wool or tweed, therefore are mainly used in offices and professional arena.

- Silk pocket squares can go to much bigger sizes than linen and cotton pocket squares can, especially if the fabric (silk) is very light. Being bigger and less stiff, they make great unstructured fold – puff, and because of its fineness, they look great on rougher jacket fabrics (wool, tweed).

- Polyester pocket squares should be avoided. They can be found very cheaply, but they also look that way. If you want to look cheap, go for it, but guessing since you picked up this book, you want to and should do better than that! That being said, some blends where there is polyester as a minor component are acceptable, but pricewise don't pay much for them (up to $10).

Winston Churchill was famous for his bow ties and pocket squares.

2. How to Wear Pocket Squares

Have you ever tried wearing a pocket square, only to find yourself being the only one in the room with one? Maybe you enjoy being at the center of attention, but many men do not have the confidence to feel comfortable wearing a pocket square. Knowing how to wear one correctly will give you the élan to wear one more often and look great doing so!

When choosing which pocket square to wear, there is one rule that must be remembered:

„Never ever wear the same color and pattern on the pocket square as on the tie."

You can be more creative than that! Let the elements of the square pick up and/or contrast other elements of your outfit. This goes for the colors as well as the pattern and texture of the material.

The combination shown here is NOT good! The first thing you should learn: Never wear the same color and pattern on the pocket square as on the tie! Photo: Amazon.com

Regarding color-coordination with pocket squares, the beauty is that there aren't many fixed rules.

„You can wear a pocket square to complement anything in your outfit, be it the color on your shirt tie, or even socks."

When matching a pocket square to color in your tie, the shirt or jacket color should be a minor or secondary color. Otherwise, the whole combination will become too matched, and that is not what we want. By the way, it is perfectly fine to wear a pocket square on the jacket without wearing a tie.

Colors can work great together either by creating contrast or harmony. Pocket squares are no exception, and should be matched either by the harmony of colors within the outfit, or by creating contrast by using complimentary colors. What are complementary colors?

Colors that are opposite to each other on the color wheel are considered to be complementary colors (example: red and green).

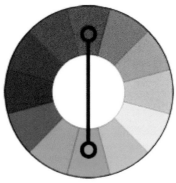

A basic color wheel. Complementary colors are always opposite each other. Image: Tigercolor.com

By choosing complementary colors, you are going for contrast. Extra care must be taken with these choices, as they can come across as jarring. The high contrast of complementary colors creates a vibrant look, especially when used at full saturation. For that reason, complementary color schemes are tricky to use in large doses, but work well when you want a small dose of color to stand out.

On the other hand, you can use analogous colors to build harmony. Analogous color schemes use colors that are next to each other on the color wheel. They usually match well and create serene and comfortable designs. Analogous color schemes are often found in nature and are harmonious and pleasing to the eye.

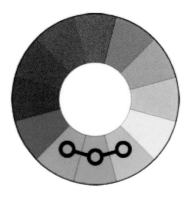

Analogous color schemes use colors that are next to each other. Image: Tigercolor.com

Therefore, when using colors next to each other on the color wheel, you are looking for harmony among the colors in your outfit. The biggest thing to watch out for is that you have enough contrast, analogous colors can easily blur together if there isn't an area with a little extra 'pop.' Choose one color to dominate and a second to support the first. The third color is used (along with black, white or gray) as an accent to create that little extra contrast and keep the look exciting.

The whole point of a pocket square is to create an interesting interplay between it and the rest of your outfit. As mentioned before, the match can be achieved either in color, pattern or texture.

In that sense, multicolored pocket squares are actually quite versatile and are nice to own as they can be worn with many colors. It is enough to pair only one color in the pocket square with anything else on your outfit.

This multicolored pocket square from Rubinacci picks up the red tone from the jacket weave. Multicolored pocket squares can be worn with many different colors. It is enough to pair only one pocket square color with anything else on your outfit. Photo: abitofcolor.tumblr.com.

For example, wearing a tie or a shirt with red stripes can call for a pocket square containing some red (remember, some red, not completely or mostly red). It should not be of a matching pattern. In this example, dots or some other printed pattern would work well. Remember, if you have already achieved a match in color, avoid other matches (such as pattern or texture), because the whole combination will look almost academically assembled.

This man is wearing three different patterns, all linked by the color blue – stripes on his shirt, dots on his tie and a more complex pattern on his pocket square. Paired with a checkered brown suit, the whole outfit looks very good. Source: abitofcolor.tumblr.com, Photo: thesartorialist.com.

Another good complement are squares with a touch of brown that pick up the color in brown shoes.

Pocket squares with a touch of brown can be a great way to pick up the color in brown shoes. In this case it is matching also the brown color in the tie and belt. Photo: Suitsupply.com

Ideally, you will want to let your neck area dominate, not your pocket square. That way, the eyes of others looking at you are drawn toward your face, not your breast pocket. The pocket square should complement your outfit, not dominate it or be too matchy or overly expressive.

„A pocket square should ideally be a different material or texture than the tie.“

If your tie is silk, a linen square will look the best; if your tie is wool or cotton, silk in the breast pocket will add the proper textural balance.

Silk pocket square with a wool jacket and tie is a good combination because the pocket square softens the rough appearance of the wool and creates balance. Photo: abitofcolor.tumblr.com

„If you have only one pocket square in your wardrobe, it should be white linen or cotton.“

This is the most classic choice, and can be combined with any suit or tie. A white cotton or linen pocket square is best worn neatly folded. All other pocket squares, especially silk, should be worn nonchalantly, tucked in your pocket as if you were not trying too hard to make it look neat. We will explore more about pocket square folds later in this book.

Why is a linen such a good fabric for a pocket square? Linen offers a bit of texture and has a crisp look that makes it look 'fresh' throughout the day. It tends to hold its shape, especially when you want perky points that will stay sharp all day long. Conversely, silk will give a softer, smoother effect.

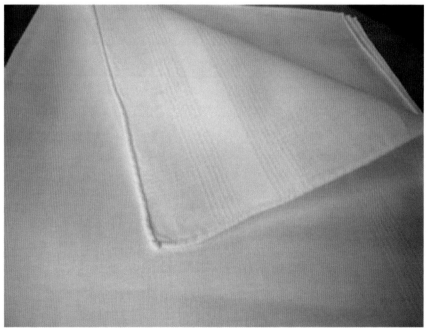

White linen pocket square. Photo: abitofcolor.tumblr.com

If you want to expand your collection beyond the basic white pocket square, look for silk pocket squares of various colors and patterns. Start with colors that will fit well into your current wardrobe and then expand to more expressive and interesting colors and patterns. There is room for your creativity to play, even in 'boring' men's formal or business clothing.

One expressive item is great. Trying to do more than that (i.e. expressive socks and an expressive pocket square) rarely works and usually clashes.

With a sedate outfit, the square alone can make all the difference. For example, a dark suit, solid blue shirt, and very discreet tie with a white pocket square is fine, but throw in a maroon paisley square and the whole look is elevated.

In some cases, you may want to avoid wearing a tie, but should still look elegant. In this case, wear just a pocket square. You will keep the formal appearance, but relieve your neck from the constriction of a tie. This definitely works for more casual events, but might even fly at work if your office doesn't have a dress code absolutely mandating a tie.

By wearing a pocket square without a tie you still keep an elegant appearance. Photo: abitofcolor.tumblr.com

Finally, remember that a pocket square is only an accessory. Like a spice in a finely prepared dish, it should add to the whole but never overpower it. Not only does it tie together multiple elements you've chosen to wear, but a pocket square is the one piece that you can really have fun with. Whether it be the fold you choose, the type of material, or even the colors, it will be the one distinguishing feature that separates you from others.

But don't forget that looking good means being properly coordinated. The wrong pocket square, tie or other accessory can really devalue the overall effect of an otherwise good outfit. Grabbing any old pocket square doesn't work, just like a haphazard choice of tie or scarf. It is a matter of coordinating colors, patterns and materials to look their best. The more practice you have in successfully coordinating elements the easier it becomes. But at first it does take effort and you will likely have some choices that work better than others.

3. How Not to Wear Pocket Squares!

1. **Don't wear woven silk pocket squares** (especially if it came in a pack with the tie of the same material or pattern!). Silk pocket squares must be light silk with pattern printed on them!

2. **Don't get too matchy.** That means, don't wear a red tie with red pocket square or a blue shirt with blue pocket square. At most, you want the square to pick up a hint of color in the tie or shirt. The more distinct the color you are picking up, the worse it looks if the square matches it exactly. Another thing to watch for is too close a match in pattern. Beyond the fact that you don't want your square to look like the tie, you also don't want its pattern to be the same scale as the pattern in the tie.

3. **Don't pick a square that gets lost against the suit.** For example a dark square will not be very visible on a dark suit. The square needs to contrast with the cloth of the suit.

4. **Don't let a lot of pocket square show from the pocket.** This is a fundamental principle: show only a little of your square. No matter what type of square it is, just let it peek out to show some color and break the monotony of the chest. If you have a monogram or a label (product label should be carefully removed before wearing the square for the first time) on your pocket square it should not show.

5. **Don't overdo it with colors.** Your livelier, more expressive squares should be reserved for otherwise sedate outfits. If you have a

lot going on elsewhere, choose a simple square. When in doubt, just wear white linen square, it goes with almost anything!

4. How to Recognize a High-Quality Pocket Square

The design of a pocket square may be plain or patterned, but for determining its quality, the most important characteristic is the design of its edges. This is the detail that gets the most attention as it is usually visible when worn.

The most expensive and highest quality pocket squares have hand-rolled and hand-stitched edges. As this requires significantly more time to sew, a pocket square with hand-rolled edges can cost much more than one whose edges are hemstitched. Luxury and custom pocket square makers take about 2 hours to make a pocket square. All edges and corners must be perfect. Edges should be stitched in a tight tube shape with approximately 5 to 6 stitches per inch. Stitching should be regularly spaced and mostly hidden.

White linen pocket squares with colored hand rolled edges. Photo: abitofcolor.tumblr.com

The finest pocket squares are made of silk or linen and always feature hand-rolled edges.

The virtue of linen is that because of its inherent stiffness, it retains its starched quality throughout the day. It is the only fabric that looks as fresh in the evening as it did in the morning when it was first folded.

In the case of printed silk pocket squares, a good print should penetrate substantially to the other side, say at least 75%. Often, both sides of your pocket square will be visible, so this is important. If you look at, for example, Hermes squares, which are considered some of the best squares in the world, you will see that they have an ink penetration level of around 90%.

Hermes silk pocket square. Photo: Hermes.com

Cheap and low quality pocket squares are usually made very quickly by a machine, having a 'rustic' edge and simple corners, or cheaply hand-rolled with loose irregular stitches. Also the fabric will be mass produced with no special characteristics. These pocket squares are often imported from China and found as the house brands in department stores. They can be priced as little as 1 dollar (on sales).

Midrange pocket squares will have better workmanship for their hand-rolled edges and nicer fabrics with interesting patterns. Many well-known brand names in large department stores and men's specialty shops will fit into this category of pocket squares. When on sale they can be a good buy even for as low as $10.

5. Where to Shop for Pocket Squares and What Prices to Expect

You don't need many pocket squares to look your very best. Focus on getting squares that complement each of your favorite jacket and tie combinations. Then, add a few fun ones for parties, dining out, etc. Also, consider a variety of materials like silk, linen, wool and cotton. Make sure you have at least one white linen square.

Any high-quality pocket square can be enjoyed for many, many years. They don't get worn out or dirty as they are only placed in your pocket and don't see any touch or strain to the material. In that sense, we suggest that you build your pocket square collection for quality, not quantity. It's better to buy a couple of high quality squares than a dozen cheap ones!

You can find a good selection of pocket squares in brick and mortar menswear stores, as well as in many online stores.

The benefits of buying pocket squares in physical stores are that you can try them on and get some advice from the sales personnel. You can also bring your jacket, shirt and/or tie to see how they match with the pocket squares available. However, buying pocket squares online can be beneficial as well. You can easily shop around, compare prices and look at many different styles and designs in just a couple of minutes from the comfort of your home. It can be a much more inexpensive option as well, as there are many good online shops competing for your attention and trust.

That said, if you want to visit some physical stores to see their offerings, don't miss Brooks Brothers, Macy's, Nordstrom, Barneys and other similar retailers selling men's clothing. You might check their websites as well.

Some recommended online stores that offer pocket squares are:

http://www.kentwang.com/pocket-squares - a small company from Austin, Texas that is dedicated to making high quality, classic menswear at reasonable prices. All of their pocket squares are hand sewn and designed in an array of styles, from austere to flamboyant. The edges on all their pocket squares are hand rolled and prices range from $20 to $35.

http://www.howardyount.com/collections/pocket-squares - founded in 2008, Howard Yount is dedicated to the uncompromising pursuit of style. Their goal is to provide high quality products with an attention to detail and high level of personal service. All their pocket squares have hand rolled edges with prices from $20 to $35.

http://www.bergbergstore.com/ - Norwegian brand making pocket squares (and other accessories for men) designed in Norway and hand made in Italy. Often they have very interesting designs. Prices of pocket squares are about EUR 20.

http://www.samhober.com – THE place to go for a custom made pocket squares! They have a huge selection and their products are first class - all hand made with hand rolled edges. They can make you a bespoke pocket square in the size of your choice from any of 100s of different fabrics they have on stock. Prices of pocket squares start at $25.

http://www.drakes-london.com/hanks - founded in 1977, today Drakes is the largest independent producer of handmade ties in England, offering also a wide range of pocket squares in linen, silk, wool, and blends of wool and silk priced at GBP 50.

http://www.pjohnsonshop.com/collections/pocket-square - custom tailors from Australia offering exquisite printed silk and blended silk/wool/cotton pocket squares, all with hand rolled edges priced at $75.

http://store.asuitablewardrobe.net/pocketsquaresandhandkerchiefs.aspx - Pocket squares found at 'A Suitable Wardrobe' are from some of the best makers in the world, including Simonnot-Godard of France, Drake's London and a couple of small Neapolitan makers. All their pocket squares are made entirely by hand in Ireland, Italy and France using cloth woven in the world's finest mills. Each edge is hand rolled and hand sewn for the finest finish and look. Prices vary from $25 to $95.

http://www.bensilver.com/Pocket-Squares.html - offers classic, refined and tasteful clothing and accessories for gentlemen who enjoy the added dash of updated color. A wide range of pocket squares can be found on their site, ranging from $18 for a plain cotton pocket square to $95 for exclusive printed silk ones.

6. How to Fold a Pocket Square

When folding your pocket squares, you can go two ways:
1. into more structured folds (like the TV fold for example) which are more serious, and
2. unstructured folds (such as the puff) which give a softer look.

Linen and cotton pocket squares are mostly worn in a structured fold, while silk and wool are usually worn in an unstructured fold.

There is no right or wrong folding style for an occasion. You can wear any fold for any occasion, only remember that structured folds are more serious and conservative, while unstructured ones are more casual, but still elegant!

The following are the most popular pocket square folds and how to fold them:

<u>Structured:</u>

TV Fold (also called 'Flat fold' 'Architect' or 'Presidential')

1. Lay your pocket square flat with the two top corners horizontal.

2. Fold the left side over the right side.

3. Fold the bottom up just short of the top.

4. Tuck as needed and place your pocket square in your jacket pocket.

One Point fold

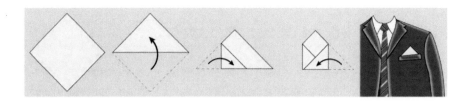

1. Lay your pocket square flat with one corner facing up and one corner facing down.

2. Fold the bottom corner up to meet the top corner.

3. Fold the left corner to the right.

4. Repeat and fold the right corner to the left.

5. Tuck as needed and place your pocket square in your jacket pocket.

Two Point fold

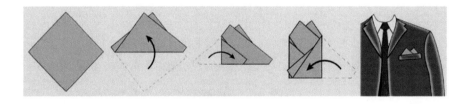

1. Lay your pocket square flat with one corner facing up and one corner facing down.

2. Fold the bottom corner up and just to the left of the top corner.

3. Fold the left side in towards the right.

4. Fold the right side in towards the left.

5. Tuck as needed and place your pocket square in your jacket pocket.

Three point fold

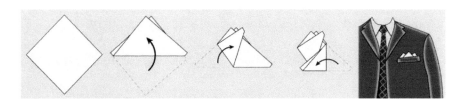

    1. Lay your pocket square flat with one corner facing up and one corner facing down.

    2. Fold the bottom corner up to the top just to the left of the top corner.

    3. Fold the left side towards the right and up to the right of the 'middle peak'.

    4. Fold the right side straight across in to the left.

    5. Tuck as needed and place your pocket square in your jacket pocket.

Unstructured:

Puff fold

    1. Lay your pocket square flat with the two top corners horizontal. Pinch the middle of the pocket square and pick it up.

    2. As you pick up the pocket square tuck the sides in as in the diagram.

    3. With one hand firmly holding the pocket square, use your other hand to gently gather it closer.

    4. Now gather up the bottom of the pocket square.

    5. Tuck as needed and place your pocket square in your jacket pocket.

(Source for folding explanations and graphics: http://www.samhober.com)

7. How to Care for Your Pocket Squares

Since pocket squares usually do not get dirty, people usually don't wash them. If for some reason you need to clean a pocket square, here are the steps you need to take so they retain their shape and color.

Pocket squares can be washed at home (carefully and by hand!) or dry cleaned by a reliable dry cleaner that has experience with fine garments (especially if the pocket square is of silk).

If you are doing it at home, use a gentle detergent or even shampoo and wash it by hand in lukewarm water. Rinse it well and hang it or place it on a flat surface to dry. Do not wring it out and do not put it in the sun. Also, do not use a dryer!

If necessary, pocket squares can also be ironed. Iron them only on the reverse side and never over the hand rolled edges. Set your iron to a low silk setting and use a press cloth between the pocket square and the iron to prevent a glossy shine from developing on the surface. You can also use steam to moisten the square so the wrinkles release more easily, but be careful not to leave water spots on the square.

Pocket squares should be stored in a dark and dry place. They can be hung, folded or just thrown in a box; they will keep their shape. For convenience, organize your collection so you can see all of your squares when choosing which one to wear!

About the Author

Mark Davids, an internet entrepreneur coming from the homeland of ties – Croatia, is the go-to person to ask about neckties, bow ties and pocket squares. He is the new, modern type of a gentleman that has years of experience in both corporate and entrepreneurial world.

Having studied marketing in the UK and having a flair for anything British, Mark likes to use accessories like neckties, bow ties and pocket squares to smart up his appearance and dress like a modern British gentleman.

Mark spends much of his time travelling around the world, meeting new cultures and places. He likes to write his books during the travels.

All of his books are the result of his own research and personal experiences from wearing these beloved accessories daily.

Mark likes to collect special ties he finds during his travels around the world, and from time to time, he auctions parts of his collection on eBay (mark_davids).

Made in the USA
Lexington, KY
17 May 2016